MW00887193

HI, MISTER SQUIRREL!

Written and Illustrated by:
Harrison Markowsky

"Morning, Buddy! Looks like we have some pretty nice weather today. My birds will be happy!" Dad said with a big smile.

"Oh look, there they go again. The squirrels are back on the bird feeder.
Shoo them away, they keep eating all my bird food." Dad looked concerned.
Out the door Buddy shouted, "What are you guys doing?
Get off of there, that's not for you, that's for the birds!"

"We need something to keep them from going up the pole.
They're not going to listen to us!" Buddy said giggling.

"How about this simple cone?
It should keep them from climbing all the way up," said Dad.

Buddy cried out, "The cone is working.
Now they can't be hogs and steal the bird food. Hungry little squirrels!"

"Hi! I see you Mister Squirrel!"

The Next Morning
"Oh, hi, Mister Squirrel! What are you doing up on the porch?
I bet you're hungry, since you can't get to the bird food now," said Buddy to
the curious squirrel.

"Ok, well maybe I can give you something to eat just this once.
Do you want a peanut?"

With a sniff and a quick inspection, the squirrel takes the
peanut to the tree, climbing onto the branch
where he begins to crack it open.

Excited, Buddy sang out, "Doot da doo! Hooray!"

Later That Same Day

Surprised, Buddy looked outside and said, "Two Misters!?
Looks like you told your friend about that peanut! Okay, last time."

"There you go!" said Buddy, tossing two peanuts to the squirrels.

The Next Morning

Giggling, Buddy asked the squirrels,
"Umm, where did you all come from! What are you all doing now!?

Let me guess... something to eat?"

"Doot da doo! Something to eat!" sang Buddy to the squirrels.

"They sure love eating!"

"Hey, look at that! You're so little and you've got a short fluffy tail!
I'm going to call you Mister Baby!"

"And look at that funny ear you have!
You're Mister Bent Ear!"

"And you've got a dark, dirty nose from all that digging.
I'll call you Mister Brownie!"

"Oh, and you are so cute and chubby with that big belly!
You can be Mister Fatty!"

The Next Morning

"Hey, where are they?" Buddy asked, looking out the window.
"Where are who, Buddy?" asked Dad.

Buddy ran outside and yelled out, asking, "Hey!? Misters!? Anyone want something to eat!? Misters!?"

"Screech!" said the hawk swooping across the lawn.
"Ahh, Ahh!" Buddy yelled back, startled.

"Get out of here Mister Hawk! These squirrels are not for you to attack,
they are my friends!" yelled Buddy, watching the hawk fly away.
"Now I know why the Misters were hiding," said Buddy to Dad.

"Okay, Misters! That scary Hawk is gone now! It's safe to come out! Misters, come get something to eat!" Buddy called out into the woods.

"Here they come. Hi Baby, hi Brownie, hi Bent Ear, hi Mister Fatty!
Don't worry, I won't let Mister Hawk hurt any of you!"

"Something to eat?!" Buddy asked again.

"Doot da doo!" replied Mister Squirrel.

Harrison Markowsky is a graphic designer and illustrator from North Andover, MA. For his senior capstone project as part of graduating from Merrimack College, he chose to write, illustrate, and publish "Hi, Mister Squirrel!"
The idea for this book came from his love of nature and from his daily interactions with the squirrels in his backyard!

For more information on Harrison Markowsky, please visit harrisonmarkowsky.com

Copyright © 2021 by Harrison Markowsky

All rights reserved. In accordance with the U.S. Copyright Act of 1976, the scanning, uploading, and electronic sharing of any part of this book without the permission of the publisher is unlawful piracy and theft of the author's intellectual property.

If you would like to use material from the book (other than for review purposes), prior written permission must be obtained by contacting the publisher. Thank you for your support of the author's rights.

CPSIA information can be obtained
at www.ICGtesting.com
Printed in the USA
BVHW022308130521
607264BV00002B/21